The Life of Bahá'u'lláh

A TREASURY OF STORIES FROM Brilliant Star

COLLECTOR'S EDITION

Celebrating the 200th Birthday of Bahá'u'lláh

Bahá'í Publishing
401 Greenleaf Avenue, Wilmette, Illinois 60091

Copyright © 2017 by the National Spiritual Assembly
of the Bahá'ís of the United States

20 19 18 17   4   3   2   1

Library of Congress Cataloging-in-Publication Data
Names: Bahá'í Publishing.
Title: The life of Bahá'u'lláh : a treasury of stories from Brilliant star.
Other titles: Brilliant star.
Description: Wilmette, IL : Bahá'í Publishing, 2017.
Identifiers: LCCN 2017023679 | ISBN 9781618511218 (alk. paper)
Subjects: LCSH: Bahá'u'lláh, 1817–1892.
Classification: LCC BP392 .L54 2017 | DDC 297.9/363 [B] —dc23
LC record available at https://lccn.loc.gov/2017023679

ABOUT THE COVER

Art by C. Aaron Kreader and
watercoloring by Lisa Blecker

The cover illustration was developed with reference to a 19th-century photograph of an outdoor market at the time when Bahá'u'lláh lived in Tihrán, Persia (now Iran). The children running toward the bazaar, full of joy and wonder, catch sight of a singing nightingale overhead.

The nightingale is a prominent symbol in the Bahá'í writings and is used to represent Bahá'u'lláh's message of peace and unity. In the Tablet of Ahmad, revealed in 1865, Bahá'u'lláh wrote, "the Nightingale of Paradise singeth upon the twigs of the Tree of Eternity, with holy and sweet melodies, proclaiming to the sincere ones the glad tidings of the nearness of God . . ."

> "My first counsel is this: Possess a pure, kindly and radiant heart..."
> — Bahá'u'lláh

MISSION OF PEACE

What if you were an agent on a critical mission, and your goal was to find the *secret* to world peace? Along the way, you could even travel through time. Bahá'ís and other friends around the world believe that the secret has been revealed!

The Bahá'í Faith was started by Bahá'u'lláh, Who was born in Persia (now Iran) in 1817. This year is the 200th anniversary of His birth.

Bahá'u'lláh taught that the world's religions are connected and come from one powerful force, like rays from one sun. Each faith was founded by a Messenger of God, such as Abraham, Buddha, Jesus, and Muhammad. God sends a new Messenger as humanity evolves and needs renewed divine guidance. Bahá'ís believe that Bahá'u'lláh is God's most recent Messenger.

During His life, Bahá'u'lláh revealed over 100 books and tablets of sacred writings. Because officials wanted to stop Him, He was imprisoned, persecuted, and exiled far from His home. But He was on a truly critical mission to share His message of unity, and He persisted. He urged us to end conflicts based on race and religion. He said women and men are equal and that all people should be educated. He asked world leaders to stop wars. Today, these ideas are embraced by millions of Bahá'ís and by people of many faiths who work for justice and peace.

So, what's the secret to peace? It's *love*. When we can see *everyone* on Earth as members of one human family and treat people with love, our actions build peace. It's not easy—sometimes the world can feel dark and worrisome. But with open minds and open hearts, we can shine the light of unity and stand up for justice together. Even when Bahá'u'lláh's life was in danger, He kept encouraging people to love each other.

We're excited for you to explore this book and travel through Bahá'u'lláh's time while discovering many ways you can shine your light. We searched through our vaults to collect some of our best treasures to celebrate the 200th anniversary of Bahá'u'lláh's birth and His mission of peace—and to empower you in *your* important mission as a world citizen.

♡ BRILLIANT STAR

CONTENTS

it can illuminate the whole earth."

— Bahá'u'lláh

Celebrating the
200th Anniversary of Bahá'u'lláh's Birth

Why are we here? How should we live our lives? What happens when we die? Throughout history, God has sent Teachers to help us answer these kinds of questions. Like Jesus, Buddha, Muhammad, and other Messengers of God before Him, Bahá'u'lláh brought divine teachings for our age. The religion He founded, the Bahá'í Faith, offers a message of peace, unity, and hope.

Bahá'u'lláh was named Mírzá Husayn-'Alí when He was born in Tihrán, Persia (now Iran), in 1817. As a child of a wealthy nobleman, He didn't attend school, yet He was remarkably wise and could talk about difficult religious teachings with Muslim leaders. "Bahá'u'lláh," the title He would later take, means "Glory of God" in Arabic.

Bahá'u'lláh was always kind and generous. As a young man, He was offered an important job in the government, but He didn't accept it.

Instead, He chose to share His time and money with those in need. People called Him "Father of the Poor."

Vision in a Dungeon

When He was 27, Bahá'u'lláh became a follower of a new Messenger of God known as the Báb, Whose name means "the Gate." The Báb taught that another Messenger would soon come to bring unity to the world.

Islamic authorities wanted to stop the Báb and His teachings. They executed Him in 1850. His followers, called Bábís, were persecuted terribly. More than 20,000 were killed.

In 1852, Bahá'u'lláh was put in heavy chains and thrown into a dungeon called the "Black Pit" with other Bábís. Each day, a Bábí was pulled from the dungeon, tortured, and executed. Bahá'u'lláh's family feared He would be killed. Their home was ransacked, and they were forced to flee.

Bahá'u'lláh spent four months in the filthy, vermin-infested Black Pit. Even in these miserable conditions, Bahá'u'lláh's spirit soared. It was during this time that He had a mystical experience that would change His life. He saw a vision of a radiant maiden, who called Bahá'u'lláh the "Best-Beloved of the worlds." He later wrote that "the breezes of the All-Glorious were wafted over Me, and taught Me the knowledge of all that hath been." After this vision, Bahá'u'lláh began to reveal holy writings.

Unstoppable Mission

When He was released from prison, Bahá'u'lláh was banished from His homeland. He went to Baghdád, Iraq. Still, He continued to share His message of unity. He taught that the human race is one family and religion should bring peace, not war. He called on all people to work for the betterment of the world.

November 12, 1817
Birth of Bahá'u'lláh in Tihrán, Iran. His home in Tihrán is shown here.

1844
Recognizes the Báb as a new Messenger of God

1852
Imprisonment in the "Black Pit" of Tihrán. The "X" marks the site of the prison.

1853–1863
Exile in Baghdád, Iraq. From 1854–1856, He goes into the mountains to pray in solitude.

April 1863
Declares Divine Mission as Prophet-Founder of the Bahá'í Faith

At right is Arabic calligraphy meaning "Yá Bahá'u'l-Abhá" or "O Thou Glory of the Most Glorious!" It refers to Bahá'u'lláh.

All men have been created to carry forward an ever-advancing civilization," He wrote. In time, He announced that He was the Messenger of God Whom the Báb had foretold.

For the rest of His life, Bahá'u'lláh lived in exile or imprisonment in what are now Iraq, Turkey, and Israel. His family shared in His sufferings. At times, they endured strenuous journeys, had very little food, lived in cramped quarters, and faced prejudice and hostility from those around them. The authorities thought that by sending Bahá'u'lláh away, they could stop His teachings from spreading.

But Bahá'u'lláh's divine mission for a peaceful world was unstoppable. His exiles only carried the seeds of His Faith even farther. Bahá'u'lláh wrote more than 100 volumes of letters, tablets, and books. When He passed away in 1892, He left a written will naming His eldest son, 'Abdu'l-Bahá, as leader of the Bahá'í Faith.

Making a Vision Real

Bahá'u'lláh's writings, along with those of the Báb and 'Abdu'l-Bahá, make up the sacred Bahá'í scriptures. The Bahá'í writings also include the words of Shoghi Effendi, 'Abdu'l-Bahá's grandson, who led the Faith after his passing, and the Universal House of Justice, the elected council that guides the Faith today.

More than five million Bahá'ís throughout the world strive to make Bahá'u'lláh's vision of one unified world a reality. They will celebrate the 200th anniversary of Bahá'u'lláh's birth in 2017, and of the Báb's birth in 2019. These twin holy days will, in the words of the House of Justice, honor "those divine Figures Who set in motion an irresistible process of individual and social change."

Bahá'u'lláh's Message of Peace

Bahá'u'lláh shared these teachings about building peace. Imagine what the world will be like when these principles are widely practiced.

- We are one human family
- The world's religions are from one God
- Prejudice must end
- Women and men are equal
- Education for all
- Economic justice
- Harmony of science and religion

1863–1868
Exile in Constantinople (Istanbul), then Adrianople (Edirne), Turkey, where He lives in this home for one year. He begins writing to kings and rulers in 1867, urging unity.

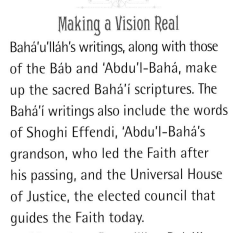

1868
Last exile to prison-city of 'Akká, Israel. After nine years, He is able to live in the countryside homes of Mazra'ih and then Bahjí, outside 'Akká.

May 29, 1892
Bahá'u'lláh passes away and is laid to rest in this shrine at Bahjí, in Israel.

October 22, 2017
Global community honors 200th anniversary of Bahá'u'lláh's birth.

The Puppet Show

A theater performance can make you laugh, cry, or want to dance and sing. As a child, Bahá'u'lláh saw a puppet show that He said changed His view of the world.

Bahá'u'lláh's father, Mírzá Buzurg, was a minister in the court of the sháh (the king). When Bahá'u'lláh was a child, one of His older brothers got married—and the festivities lasted for seven days! On the last day, a puppet show was performed for the guests' entertainment.

Bahá'u'lláh watched eagerly as the show began. Human-like puppets called, "His Majesty is coming! Arrange the seats at once!" They quickly prepared for the puppet king's arrival. More puppets gathered—noblemen, soldiers, and servants of the king's royal court.

Finally, the king made a grand entrance wearing a magnificent crown, and he proudly sat on his high throne. Trumpets sounded, and a thief was brought before the court. The king ordered his execution. Immediately, the thief was put to death! Then the king learned that a rebellion had broken out. He sent his army into battle, and cannons were fired. Bahá'u'lláh watched the scene "with great amazement."

After the show ended, a man came out from behind the scenery, carrying a box.

"What is this box," Bahá'u'lláh asked him, "and what was the nature of this display?"

The man replied, "All this lavish display and these elaborate devices, the king, the princes, and the ministers, their pomp and glory, their might and power, everything you saw, are now contained within this box."

From that day on, Bahá'u'lláh said, He saw worldly power as no more important

When Bahá'u'lláh was a child, a puppet show called *Sháh Sultán Salím* was performed for His family and their guests, who included princes and other leaders.

than a puppet show. He wrote, "All the trappings of the world . . . have never been, nor will they ever be, of any weight and consequence, be it to the extent of a grain of mustard seed . . . These visible treasures, these earthly vanities, these arrayed armies . . . all shall pass into the confines of the grave, as though into that box."

In 1839, when Mírzá Buzurg passed away, Bahá'u'lláh was offered His father's position at court. But Bahá'u'lláh turned it down. Instead, He spent His time serving people in need and sharing His wealth with them.

Bahá'u'lláh later proclaimed His message of peace. Trying to stop Him, the authorities persecuted, imprisoned, and exiled Him. He lost His wealth. But as the puppet show from His childhood had shown, He knew that only spiritual wealth lasts. He wrote to kings and rulers of His day, urging them to stop injustice and establish peace. Today, Bahá'ís around the globe work to put Bahá'u'lláh's teachings into practice and help build global justice and unity.

Gift of Love

A Brief Timeline

The Life of Bahá'u'lláh

The highlighted area marks the time in which this story takes place.

1817 November 12
Birth of Bahá'u'lláh in Tihrán, Iran

1844
Recognizes the Báb as a new Messenger of God

1852
Imprisonment in the "Black Pit" of Tihrán

1853–1863
Exile in Baghdád, Iraq. From 1854–1856, He goes into the mountains to pray in solitude.

1863 April
Declares Divine Mission as Prophet-Founder of the Bahá'í Faith

1863–1868
Exile in Constantinople (Istanbul), then Adrianople (Edirne), Turkey. Begins writing letters to kings and rulers in 1867, urging world unity

1868
Last exile, to prison-city of 'Akká, Israel

1877
Finally free to live in countryside homes of Mazra'ih and then Bahjí, outside 'Akká

1892 May 29
Bahá'u'lláh passes away at Bahjí.

As the son of a nobleman in Persia (now Iran), Bahá'u'lláh could have spent His young adulthood living a life of luxury. But He chose to use His time and wealth to help the poor.

One day in 1844, when He was about 27, a student brought Him a scroll. It contained writings of the Báb, a Messenger of God Who taught that another Messenger would soon appear to bring an age of peace. The scroll had been sent by Mullá Husayn, the Báb's first follower, who had heard of Bahá'u'lláh's selfless work.

As Bahá'u'lláh read the Báb's words aloud, the student was "enraptured" by "the sound of His voice and the sweetness of its melody." Bahá'u'lláh praised the Báb's "soul-stirring words" and said they had "regenerating power." He gave the student tea and some special sugar—rare gifts in Persia at that time—to take to Mullá Husayn, along with His appreciation and love. Mullá Husayn received the gifts with enthusiasm.

Bahá'u'lláh soon set out to share the Báb's teachings. He went to His family's home in the district of Núr and conveyed the new faith to people with eloquence. He became a leader among the Bábís.

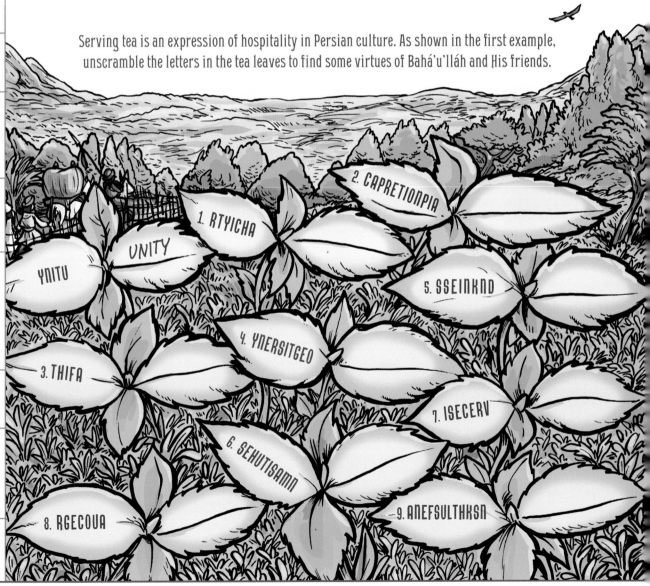

Serving tea is an expression of hospitality in Persian culture. As shown in the first example, unscramble the letters in the tea leaves to find some virtues of Bahá'u'lláh and His friends.

1. RTYICHA
2. CAPRETIONPIA
UNITY — YNITU
3. THIFA
4. YNERSITGEO
5. SSEINKND
6. SEHUTISAMN
7. ISECERV
8. RGECOUA
9. ANEFSULTHKSN

A Brief
Timeline

The Life of
Bahá'u'lláh

The highlighted
area marks the
time in which this
story takes place.

Spiritual Riches

Although Bahá'u'lláh and His wife, Ásíyih Khánum, came from wealthy families, they weren't attached to material things. They were happy to generously share their riches with those in need.

When Bahá'u'lláh was arrested due to His beliefs as a Bábí, He and His family were stripped of their wealth and then banished from their homeland. For about 40 years, Bahá'u'lláh lived as a prisoner and an exile, with few comforts.

Yet He was rich with admirers. Sometimes they sent Him gifts, such as carpets or clothes.

He graciously accepted the gifts, but often gave them to the poor.

During His exile in Adrianople (now Edirne, Turkey), a Bahá'í named Muhammad-Báqir presented Bahá'u'lláh with a small silk rug. Bahá'u'lláh accepted the gift, wrote a tablet, and thanked him. Then He told Muhammad-Báqir that He was returning the rug as a favor to him. He said He actually preferred to sit on the ground.

Though He experienced wealth and poverty, Bahá'u'lláh was detached from both. Instead, He focused on spiritual riches, helping people live as one human family.

Carpet weaving is an art form in many cultures, including in Iran. Some carpets are used for prayer.
Imagine you're giving a beautiful carpet as a gift. Create your own design with unique patterns and colors.

A Brief
Timeline

The Life of
Bahá'u'lláh

The highlighted
area marks the
time in which this
story takes place.

United in Love and Respect

What if your family were suddenly thrust into poverty and exiled from your homeland? When Bahá'u'lláh's family endured these and many other challenges, they supported one another with love and devotion.

The children of Bahá'u'lláh and Navváb (left to right): Bahíyyih Khánum, Mírzá Mihdí, and 'Abdu'l-Bahá. They dedicated their lives to their family and their faith's message of peace.

Bahá'u'lláh was nearly 18 years old when He married Ásíyih Khánum in Tihrán, Persia (now Iran), in 1835. She was noble and intelligent, with striking, dark blue eyes. Unlike most girls in Persia at the time, she was educated. They both came from wealthy families and could have chosen a life of ease. But they gave generous help to those in need. Bahá'u'lláh was called "Father of the Poor" and Ásíyih Khánum "Mother of Consolation."

Bahá'u'lláh honored Ásíyih Khánum with the title "Navváb," meaning "Highness" or "Grace." Women were usually not treated as equals, but their relationship was one of mutual respect and love. Their eldest son, 'Abbás Effendi, later took the name 'Abdu'l-Bahá, or "Servant of Bahá." They also had a daughter, Bahíyyih Khánum, and a younger son, Mírzá Mihdí.

The family's life changed dramatically in 1852, when Bahá'u'lláh was unjustly imprisoned because of His faith. Their home was plundered, and most of their possessions were taken. Navváb and her children, who were all under nine, struggled to survive while they worried about Bahá'u'lláh's safety. At one point, Navváb could only offer her children a handful of dry flour to eat.

After Bahá'u'lláh was released from prison, He was exiled to Baghdád, Iraq. This marked the beginning of many years of terrible difficulties for the family, yet they remained united and courageous.

Bahá'u'lláh's final exile led the family to 'Akká, in what is now Israel, in 1868. There, Mírzá Mihdí, at the age of 22, died after a fall. Because they were prisoners, the family could not go to the cemetery for his burial.

In 1877, Bahá'u'lláh was finally allowed to move to a home in the countryside. 'Abdu'l-Bahá remained in 'Akká, where he met with officials on his Father's behalf and helped to lead the Bahá'í community. Bahá'u'lláh revealed His holy writings and met with Bahá'ís. He praised 'Abdu'l-Bahá, whom He called "the Master," saying, "For Us He has become a mighty stronghold, a mighty armour." *

Throughout her life, Bahíyyih Khánum also served her Father and the Bahá'í Faith with kindness, strength, and wisdom.

When Navváb passed away in 1886, Bahá'u'lláh, 'Abdu'l-Bahá, and Bahíyyih Khánum were at her side. Today, Bahá'ís pray at the resting places of Navváb and her children on Mount Carmel in Haifa, Israel.

*This quote is from a Bahá'í's autobiography and may not reflect Bahá'u'lláh's exact words.

Champion of Oneness

The Life of Bahá'u'lláh

The highlighted area marks the time in which this story takes place.

1817 November 12
Birth of Bahá'u'lláh in Tihrán, Iran

1844
Recognizes the Báb as a new Messenger of God

1852
Imprisonment in the "Black Pit" of Tihrán

1853–1863
Exile in Baghdád, Iraq. From 1854–1856, He goes into the mountains to pray in solitude.

1863 April
Declares Divine Mission as Prophet-Founder of the Bahá'í Faith

1863–1868
Exile in Constantinople (Istanbul), then Adrianople (Edirne), Turkey. Begins writing letters to kings and rulers in 1867, urging world unity

1868
Last exile, to prison-city of 'Akká, Israel

1877
Finally free to live in countryside homes of Mazra'ih and then Bahjí, outside 'Akká

1892 May 29
Bahá'u'lláh passes away at Bahjí.

Throughout His life, Bahá'u'lláh endured prejudice and persecution. Still, He shared His vision for peace and unity on Earth.

As a young man in Tihrán, Persia (now Iran), Bahá'u'lláh was a devoted follower of the Báb. Bahá'u'lláh shared the Báb's message with others, and many became Bábís.

Thousands embraced the Bábí Faith across the land. But the Muslim clergy and authorities felt threatened by the new faith. Many Bábís were fiercely attacked.

In northern Persia, 313 Bábís had to defend themselves from government soldiers at the shrine of Shaykh Tabarsí. Bahá'u'lláh and some companions tried to bring supplies to the Bábís there in December 1848. The group was arrested by guards. When Bahá'u'lláh asked to be punished in place of those with Him, He was tortured by having the soles of His feet beaten with a rod.

For eight months, the Bábís at Shaykh Tabarsí survived attacks by 12,000 soldiers. Finally, the army deviously proposed a truce. When the Bábís trustingly left the shrine, they were massacred.

The Báb Himself was martyred by a firing squad in Tabríz in 1850. In spite of danger, Bahá'u'lláh and others continued to support the Bábí Faith and its followers in both Persia and Iraq.

In 1852, Bahá'u'lláh was chained to other Bábís and imprisoned in a foul dungeon in Tihrán. His feet were placed in stocks and a huge chain hung around His neck. Each day, a Bábí was taken out and executed. The executioner was friendly to Bahá'u'lláh and would describe the joy

At this mosque in Amul, Persia (now Iran), Bahá'u'lláh was arrested and beaten in 1848 for being a follower of the Báb.

with which each person had faced the end of his life.

One night in a dream, Bahá'u'lláh heard these words: "Verily, We shall render Thee victorious by Thyself and by Thy Pen. Grieve Thou not for that which hath befallen Thee, neither be Thou afraid, for Thou art in safety." After four months, He was released, but He and His family were exiled from Persia to Baghdád, Iraq.

Bahá'u'lláh inspired the Bábí community in Baghdád and revealed sacred writings. In 1863, He announced the joyous news that He was the Messenger of God promised by the Báb. His followers became known as Bahá'ís.

Bahá'u'lláh was banished to Turkey, then sent to the prison-city of 'Akká, in what is now Israel. Though He faced injustice, Bahá'u'lláh focused on helping the world and promoting harmony.

He wrote to kings and leaders, advising them to end war and treat people fairly. Toward the end of His life, Bahá'u'lláh met a British scholar, Edward G. Browne, the only westerner known to have visited Him. Bahá'u'lláh told him, "These fruitless strifes, these ruinous wars shall pass away, and the 'Most Great Peace' shall come . . . Let not a man glory in this, that he loves his country; let him rather glory in this, that he loves his kind . . ."

The Shrine of Bahá'u'lláh, located near 'Akká, Israel, is considered the holiest spot on Earth to Bahá'ís.

Use the key to decode Bahá'u'lláh's words about unity.

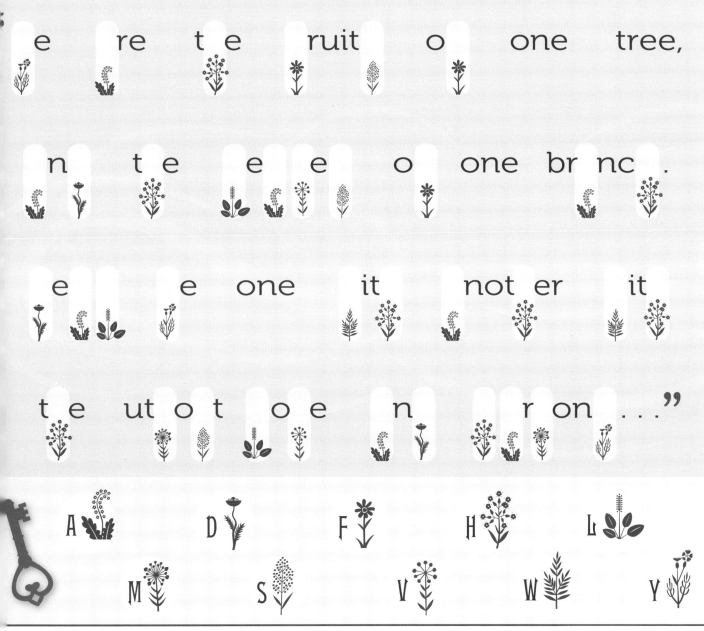

Finding Light in the Darkness

The Life of Bahá'u'lláh

The highlighted area marks the time in which this story takes place.

1817 November 12
Birth of Bahá'u'lláh in Tihrán, Iran

1844
Recognizes the Báb as a new Messenger of God

1852
Imprisonment in the "Black Pit" of Tihrán

1853–1863
Exile in Baghdád, Iraq. From 1854–1856, He goes into the mountains to pray in solitude.

1863 April
Declares Divine Mission as Prophet-Founder of the Bahá'í Faith

1863–1868
Exile in Constantinople (Istanbul), then Adrianople (Edirne), Turkey. Begins writing letters to kings and rulers in 1867, urging world unity

1868
Last exile, to prison-city of 'Akká, Israel

1877
Finally free to live in countryside homes of Mazra'ih and then Bahjí, outside 'Akká

1892 May 29
Bahá'u'lláh passes away at Bahjí.

Picture a gloomy, filthy dungeon with a horrible stench. Deep underground, it's miserably cold and crawling with vermin, such as insects or rodents. In 1852, Bahá'u'lláh was thrown into such a terrible prison in Tihrán, Persia (now Iran). It was called the Síyáh-Chál, or the "Black Pit." Bahá'u'lláh was not a criminal, but a follower of the Bábí Faith, a new religion founded by a Messenger of God known as the Báb.

Persian officials wanted to stop the Báb's teachings from spreading, because they believed they were a threat to the Islamic clergy and government. They arrested and executed Him and many of His followers. When some Bábí youth attacked the sháh (the king) in revenge for the Báb's martyrdom, abuse toward all Bábís increased. Although Bahá'u'lláh was not involved in the attack of the sháh, He and other innocent Bábís were imprisoned in the Black Pit.

Bahá'u'lláh described the prison as "a place foul beyond comparison." Many prisoners, including thieves and murderers, were crowded with Bahá'u'lláh and the other Bábís, most with no clothes or bedding. Bahá'u'lláh's feet were placed in stocks, and at all times He was forced to wear one of two heavy chains around His neck— one weighed about 112 pounds (51 kg)! For three days and nights, He had no food or drink. Later, some of His food was poisoned by those who wanted to kill Him.

Through these hardships, Bahá'u'lláh and the other Bábís remained patient. Bahá'u'lláh taught them to sing, "God is sufficient unto me; He verily is the All-sufficing! In Him let the trusting trust."

Prisoners of the "Black Pit" were chained and led through a dark corridor, then deep underground.

The sound of their voices echoed through the dungeon and amazed the sháh, who heard them from his palace near the prison.

Each day, guards called a Bábí to be executed. When unchained, he would leap to his feet, embrace Bahá'u'lláh and the other Bábís, and go to his martyrdom with courage.

It was here, in the darkest place imaginable, that Bahá'u'lláh had a wondrous spiritual experience. He said, "I felt as if something flowed from the crown of My head over My breast, even as a mighty torrent . . ." In a vision, He heard a sweet voice, and saw a maiden who pointed her finger at His head and said, "By God! This is the Best-Beloved of the worlds . . . This is the Mystery of God and His Treasure . . ."

Bahá'u'lláh's vision was the birth of a new religion, the Bahá'í Faith. He was the Messenger of God promised by the Báb. About 10 years would pass before He would announce His station.

After four months in prison, Bahá'u'lláh was exiled from Persia. But He and His teachings endured, and His message of unity and peace spread throughout the world.

Happiness During Hardship

"Those who beheld Him were assured of His great happiness," 'Abdu'l-Bahá said of his Father, Bahá'u'lláh, "for no trace of sadness or sorrow was ever visible upon His face."

But Bahá'u'lláh's happiness was not a result of an easy, carefree life. Instead, He endured about 40 years of imprisonment and exile by unjust officials who wanted to stop His teachings of unity and peace.

Bahá'u'lláh's intense hardships began in 1852, when authorities imprisoned Him for His faith. Then He was exiled from His home in Persia (now Iran) and sent to Baghdád, Iraq.

In the next 15 years, Bahá'u'lláh was exiled three more times. He and His family traveled through bitter cold and snow without adequate clothing, and through torturous heat. In 1868, Bahá'u'lláh's final exile took Him to the prison-city of 'Akká, in what is now Israel.

Surrounded by stone walls, 'Akká was dirty, with no clean water. Vicious rumors had been spread about Bahá'u'lláh and His followers, and they were met with jeers by the townspeople. For about two years, they were confined to an old army barracks.

But as 'Abdu'l-Bahá said, Bahá'u'lláh "endured all in perfect joy and happiness." In time, Bahá'u'lláh was transferred to various homes in the city. The people and officials of 'Akká grew to respect Him, His family, and His followers.

One day, Bahá'u'lláh noted that He had not seen any greenery—not a single tree or blade of grass—for nine years! 'Abdu'l-Bahá knew how much Bahá'u'lláh loved nature.

Conditions eased enough for 'Abdu'l-Bahá to venture outside the city walls. He rented a lush garden for Bahá'u'lláh. Bahá'u'lláh called it the Garden of Ridván, which means "Paradise" in Arabic. 'Abdu'l-Bahá also rented a house called Mazra'ih in the countryside near 'Akká.

Although Bahá'u'lláh was still officially a prisoner, He had become so admired that a leading official of 'Akká pleaded with Him to leave the prison-city. In June 1877, He left 'Akká to live at Mazra'ih.

Top left: Bahá'u'lláh entered 'Akká (in what is now Israel) through this sea gate. Above: Mazra'ih, Bahá'u'lláh's first home outside the prison-city of 'Akká

Bahá'u'lláh relished the beauty of Mazra'ih after His long confinement. He also enjoyed the Garden of Ridván. Bahá'ís brought trees, plants, and flowering shrubs from Persia and other countries to plant in the garden, including some rare species.

In 1879, Bahá'u'lláh moved to a home known as Bahjí ("Delight" in Arabic). He spent His final years meeting with Bahá'ís and writing about how to build peace in the world. He wrote, "Be as a lamp unto them that walk in darkness, a joy to the sorrowful . . ."

Exile to Baghdád

In December of 1852, Bahá'u'lláh had been cast into a terrible prison because of His faith. In addition to being deprived of His freedom, He was subjected to a filthy, stench-filled, pitch-dark dungeon crawling with pests, and was given little food and water. He endured the appalling conditions while tortured by stocks and massive chains.

Bahá'u'lláh was ill and exhausted when He was finally freed after four months. Then He was forced to leave Persia in a month's time. It was the dead of winter, and a month wasn't long enough to recover and prepare for the journey. His wife, Navváb, sold the few valuables she had to pay for supplies. Because His home had been destroyed, Bahá'u'lláh no longer had a home of His own, so He stayed with relatives.

On January 12, 1853, Bahá'u'lláh set out for Baghdád, Iraq, with His family and two officials. His eldest son, 'Abbás (later known as 'Abdu'l-Bahá) was eight years old, and His daughter, Bahíyyih, was six. The youngest, Mírzá Mihdí, wasn't well enough to make the journey safely, so he stayed behind with relatives. He joined his parents some years later.

Today, you can easily travel the 545 miles (877 km) from Tihrán to Baghdád within a day. But at that time, traveling by mule and on horseback, the trip took three months!

The exiles trekked through snowy mountains with little protection from the bitter temperatures. Some nights they had to camp outside, and other times they stayed in a simple stone inn with no beds. 'Abbás got frostbite. "The cold is so intense

A view of Tihrán, Persia (now Iran), where Bahá'u'lláh was imprisoned for His faith in 1852.

that one cannot even speak," Bahá'u'lláh wrote, "and ice and snow so abundant that it is impossible to move."

No light was allowed in the inns, and they had little food. One night Navváb managed to get a little flour, and she tried to make a sweet cake for Bahá'u'lláh, Who was still weakened from His ordeal in prison. But in the dark, when she reached for sugar, she picked up salt instead. Even this small treat couldn't be eaten.

The exiles persevered, and Bahá'u'lláh was treated with kindness everywhere He stopped along the way. People offered Him gifts, which He gently refused. In the village of Karand, Persia, the governor greeted Him with reverence.

As the travelers reached the border of Iraq, they rented an orchard as a place of rest. It was nearly Naw-Rúz, the Persian

> *"Blessed are the steadfastly enduring, they that are patient under ills and hardships, who lament not over anything that befalleth them . . ."* — Bahá'u'lláh

New Year. In that tranquil spot, spring flowers bloomed, water babbled in the brooks, and birds sang sweetly for the weary exiles. Bahá'u'lláh told the group that everything His enemies had planned had come to nothing.

Indeed, Bahá'u'lláh's influence was unstoppable. He later announced in Baghdád that He was the Messenger of God that the Báb had foretold. Today, followers of His teachings of peace live in virtually every country in the world.

Bahá'ís walked together toward the Shrine of Bahá'u'lláh in 'Akká, Israel, during an international convention in 2008. Bahá'u'lláh's body was laid to rest here in 1892. It's a place of pilgrimage for Bahá'ís from around the world.

Find words related to the story. Look up, down, backward, forward, and diagonally.

BAGHDAD
COLD
COMPANIONS
COURAGE
DUNGEON
EXILE
HOMELAND
JOURNEY
KINDNESS
MESSENGER
MOUNTAINS
ORCHARD
PEACE
REVERENCE
SNOW
SPRING
TIHRAN
TRAVEL
WEARY
WINTER

```
J  G  O  U  X  T  H  F  Z  S  O  A  Z  S  E
U  R  V  S  N  I  A  T  N  U  O  M  P  D  F
G  A  E  G  A  R  U  O  C  B  K  R  F  G  E
I  Y  K  V  P  Z  I  H  G  X  I  Z  H  O  R
M  E  S  S  E  N  G  E  R  N  N  A  O  C  B
V  N  D  F  A  R  B  A  G  H  D  A  D  H  U
U  R  Y  P  C  E  E  B  M  L  N  L  U  J  O
Z  U  M  N  E  L  D  N  A  L  E  M  O  H  P
W  O  B  I  I  H  R  U  C  R  S  V  L  C  H
C  J  W  X  I  Z  A  E  N  E  S  K  A  Y  F
F  K  E  N  A  R  H  I  T  G  D  S  H  R  A
B  I  A  M  N  K  C  T  Z  N  E  N  H  G  T
I  P  R  A  C  W  R  C  M  C  I  O  E  P  D
A  Y  Y  R  Q  H  O  E  L  M  S  W  N  G  G
X  V  U  G  G  C  H  S  D  U  H  W  N  O  R
```

In the Wilderness

The Life of Bahá'u'lláh

The highlighted area marks the time in which this story takes place.

1817 November 12
Birth of Bahá'u'lláh in Tihrán, Iran

1844
Recognizes the Báb as a new Messenger of God

1852
Imprisonment in the "Black Pit" of Tihrán

1853–1863
Exile in Baghdád, Iraq. From 1854–1856, He goes into the mountains to pray in solitude.

1863 April
Declares Divine Mission as Prophet-Founder of the Bahá'í Faith

1863–1868
Exile in Constantinople (Istanbul), then Adrianople (Edirne), Turkey. Begins writing letters to kings and rulers in 1867, urging world unity

1868
Last exile, to prison-city of 'Akká, Israel

1877
Finally free to live in countryside homes of Mazra'ih and then Bahjí, outside 'Akká

1892 May 29
Bahá'u'lláh passes away at Bahjí.

What do you do when faced with a troubling challenge? You can talk to someone you trust. Or you can pray and reflect for a while.

Bahá'u'lláh spent time in the wilderness, praying and meditating. He had arrived in Baghdád, Iraq, in 1853, after being banished from Persia (now Iran) by authorities who felt threatened by a growing Bábí Faith.

Bahá'u'lláh followed the teachings of the Báb. When the Báb was executed in 1850, many of His followers turned to Bahá'u'lláh for leadership. However, Bahá'u'lláh's half-brother, Mírzá Yahyá, grew jealous. He began spreading lies about Bahá'u'lláh, creating confusion and division.

This deeply saddened Bahá'u'lláh. He didn't want to be part of anything that caused disunity. So on April 10, 1854, He left His home for the mountains of Kurdistán. He dressed like a dervish—a poor, devout man who focuses on prayer. He walked about 200 miles (322 km) from Baghdád and lived simply. He said, "Many a night We had no food for sustenance, and many a day Our body found no rest . . . Alone, We communed with Our spirit . . ." He also wrote, "I shunned all else but God, and closed Mine eyes to all except Him, that haply the fire of hatred may die down and the heat of jealousy abate."

One day, Bahá'u'lláh went to a village and saw a sad boy sitting alone and crying. Bahá'u'lláh asked him what was wrong. The

Bahá'u'lláh retreated to the mountains of Kurdistán. At times He lived in a cave or a simple stone shelter.

Bahá'u'lláh used this reed pen and ink spoon when writing calligraphy.

boy said he had no copy of calligraphy to use for practicing his writing. He was afraid to return to school.

Bahá'u'lláh kindly told the boy to dry his tears. Then He wrote some words and showed him how to copy them. The boy went happily back to school. When the instructor saw Bahá'u'lláh's exquisite handwriting, he knew it was not the penmanship of an ordinary dervish. Bahá'u'lláh had learned the art of calligraphy as a child, like many who grew up in noble families.

People began to seek out the mysterious hermit who lived in the mountains. Scholars at a nearby school admired His wisdom. After about two years, Bahá'u'lláh returned to Baghdád, bringing joy to His family and friends.

> "The one object of Our retirement was to avoid becoming a subject of discord among the faithful . . . or the cause of sorrow to any heart." —Bahá'u'lláh

Bahá'u'lláh inspired unity and devotion in the Bábí community. He uplifted countless hearts in Baghdád with His compassion. Still, officials exiled Him again in 1863. Bahá'u'lláh departed Baghdád with dignity, while Mírzá Yahyá fled the city in disguise. Before He left, Bahá'u'lláh made the announcement that He was the promised Messenger of God foretold by the Báb. That day marked the birth of the Bahá'í Faith, which now has over five million followers around the globe.

Bahá'u'lláh spent 12 days in a garden on the banks of the Tigris River in Baghdád, where He announced His mission as a Messenger of God.

Bahá'u'lláh revealed His holy writings in Persian and Arabic. These languages are written in calligraphy, a widely admired art form. Traditionally, the pen (*qalam*) is made from a dried reed. Its flexibility allows the writer to make graceful, sweeping lines. Today, many people use a calligraphy marker with a slanted tip. Practice writing the Arabic word *salam* (peace). Arabic is read from right to left, so start at the right side of the page. Hold the pen very gently in your hand, and follow the numbered arrows.

A Brief Timeline

The Life of Bahá'u'lláh

The highlighted area marks the time in which this story takes place.

1817 November 12
Birth of Bahá'u'lláh in Tihrán, Iran

1844
Recognizes the Báb as a new Messenger of God

1852
Imprisonment in the "Black Pit" of Tihrán

1853–1863
Exile in Baghdád, Iraq. From 1854–1856, He goes into the mountains to pray in solitude.

1863 April
Declares Divine Mission as Prophet-Founder of the Bahá'í Faith

1863–1868
Exile in Constantinople (Istanbul), then Adrianople (Edirne), Turkey. Begins writing letters to kings and rulers in 1867, urging world unity

1868
Last exile, to prison-city of 'Akká, Israel

1877
Finally free to live in countryside homes of Mazra'ih and then Bahjí, outside 'Akká

1892 May 29
Bahá'u'lláh passes away at Bahjí.

Gifts from the Heart

As a child, Bahá'u'lláh led a life of comfort and ease. His father was a nobleman in Persia (now Iran), and His family had great wealth. Bahá'u'lláh grew up accustomed to grand homes, expensive furnishings, and fine clothing.

You might think that someone who was raised in such luxury would struggle when faced with sudden poverty. But Bahá'u'lláh was never attached to earthly riches. When His father passed away, Bahá'u'lláh was offered his prestigious position in the government, but He turned it down. He had no desire for status. Instead, He focused on helping the poor. His generosity and kindness were known throughout the area.

In 1852, things changed drastically for Bahá'u'lláh and His family. He was imprisoned for being a follower of the Báb, Whose religion was growing in Persia. The Báb's followers were persecuted terribly by the government authorities, who felt threatened by the faith. Bahá'u'lláh's wife, Navváb, who also came from a wealthy family, had to leave their home and hide in the city with their children.

After Bahá'u'lláh was released, He was exiled from Persia. For the next 40 years, He lived a simple life, often with little food or clothing. But He was never sad that His valuables were gone. In fact, when He received gifts, He gave them away! At one time, His only luxury was a small prayer rug, but He sold it when His followers needed money. And when people came to visit, Bahá'u'lláh always shared whatever He had, such as oranges, roses, sweet candy, and delicious cups of tea.

Bahá'ís around the globe strive to follow Bahá'u'lláh's example, as well as His teachings, by being detached from material things. He taught that extremes of poverty and wealth should be avoided, and all of the members of our human family should be treated with compassion and justice.

"They who are possessed of riches, however, must have the utmost regard for the poor, for great is the honor destined by God for those poor who are steadfast in patience . . ." He wrote, "and well is it with the rich who bestow their riches on the needy and prefer them before themselves."

For over two years, Bahá'u'lláh was confined to this prison in 'Akká, Israel, with about 70 family members and followers. The two windows at top right gave Him His only view of the outside world.

"To give and to be generous are attributes of Mine; well is it with
him that adorneth himself with My virtues." —Bahá'u'lláh

Find 12 things that Bahá'u'lláh happily shared or gave away. Look for words going up, down, forward, backward, and diagonally. After you've found them all, the remaining letters — in order from left to right — will form the words in the quote by Bahá'u'lláh.

Beautiful Book   Jeweled Sword   Prayer Rug
Candy   Orange   Roses
Coins   Perfume   Shawl
Cup of Tea   Prayer Beads   Shirt

```
J P K E O A O R S S
E A O G S E S O R H
W V O N S T E A W I
E O B A D F N E D R
L G L R A O R M O T
E U U O E P S U S G
D I F R B U F F N T
S C I E R C N R I D
W A T S E E I E O T
O N U H Y W Y P C I
R D A A A L L A M A
D Y E W R K E T R H
E E B L P R I C H P
```

"To be _ _ _ _ in all _ _ _ _ _ God is _ _ _ _ _ _ _ _ _

_ _ _ _ _ ...for in the _ _ _ _ _ _ _ _ _ _ _ _ _ _

_ _ _ _ _ _ _ _ _ in God." —Bahá'u'lláh

Changing Enemies to Friends

The highlighted
area marks the
time in which this
story takes place.

If you heard that over 100 people were coming to harm you because of your faith, what would you do?

Bahá'u'lláh faced such threats and persecution throughout His life. When He was 27, He became a follower of the Báb, a Messenger of God who taught that a Promised One would soon appear to unite the world. Trying to stop Bahá'u'lláh's influence as a Bábí leader, government authorities imprisoned Him in 1852. They later exiled Him from Persia (now Iran) to Baghdád, Iraq.

In Baghdád, Bahá'u'lláh often met with townspeople in coffee houses and shared the Báb's teachings. He was admired by many, but some influential leaders opposed Him. They tried to turn people against Him by spreading vicious rumors. A religious leader accused Him of trying to destroy the Muslim faith. A government official even plotted to have Him killed.

The Bábís feared for Bahá'u'lláh's life and watched His house at night. But Bahá'u'lláh showed no fear. He continued to go out at all hours. When He met His enemies, He talked and joked with them. A concerned friend suggested that He hide at home, but He wrote, "We have lighted the fire of love . . . We shall not run away, We shall not endeavor to repel the stranger . . ."

One day, a Turkish man named Ridá aimed a pistol at Bahá'u'lláh from a distance. But when Bahá'u'lláh appeared, Ridá became so confused that he dropped his gun and froze. Bahá'u'lláh said to His brother, who was with Him, "Pick up his pistol and give it

Bahá'u'lláh lived in this house during much of His time in Baghdád. It was confiscated in the 1900s and illegally destroyed in 2013.

to him, and show him the way to his house; he seems to have lost his way."

A friend warned Bahá'u'lláh that a group of more than 100 was planning an assault on His house. The Bábís gathered to defend Him, but Bahá'u'lláh said there was no need for action.

When the fierce mob arrived, rather than hide or flee, Bahá'u'lláh invited them into His home! "They are our guests," He said. He had rosewater sherbet and tea served to them. They arrived as enemies, but after experiencing Bahá'u'lláh's kindness, they left as friends.

An angry mob went to Bahá'u'lláh's house.

The authorities, however, continued to plot against Bahá'u'lláh and push for Him to leave Baghdád. In 1863, He was sent by the Turkish government to Constantinople (now Istanbul).

Before He left, Bahá'u'lláh announced that He was the Promised One that the Báb had foretold. More adversaries challenged Him throughout His life, but He continued to face them all with love and courage.

The spoken quotations from Bahá'u'lláh may not have been His exact words.

Majestic Presence

The Life of
Bahá'u'lláh

The highlighted area marks the time in which this story takes place.

1817 November 12
Birth of Bahá'u'lláh in Tihrán, Iran

1844
Recognizes the Báb as a new Messenger of God

1852
Imprisonment in the "Black Pit" of Tihrán

1853–1863
Exile in Baghdád, Iraq. From 1854–1856, He goes into the mountains to pray in solitude.

1863 April
Declares Divine Mission as Prophet-Founder of the Bahá'í Faith

1863–1868
Exile in Constantinople (Istanbul), then Adrianople (Edirne), Turkey. Begins writing letters to kings and rulers in 1867, urging world unity

1868
Last exile, to prison-city of 'Akká, Israel

1877
Finally free to live in countryside homes of Mazra'ih and then Bahjí, outside 'Akká

1892 May 29
Bahá'u'lláh passes away at Bahjí.

Imagine how it would feel to meet a Messenger of God in person. A Persian prince who knew Bahá'u'lláh said, "I know not how to explain it . . . were all the sorrows of the world to be crowded into my heart they would, I feel, all vanish, when in the presence of Bahá'u'lláh. It is as if I had entered Paradise itself."

In Bahá'u'lláh's time, many people went to coffee houses to talk about religion and philosophy. He visited these places often, and crowds gathered to see Him.

Though He suffered imprisonment and banishment, Bahá'u'lláh's kindness, generosity, and wisdom brought joy to people's hearts everywhere He went. Still, authorities who felt threatened by Bahá'u'lláh exiled Him from Persia (now Iran) to Baghdád, Iraq, in 1853. Bahá'u'lláh was a follower of an earlier Messenger of God known as the Báb. The authorities mistakenly thought the Báb's teachings went against Islam, and they persecuted thousands of His followers, called Bábís.

Bahá'u'lláh had a strong effect on the people of Baghdád. Religious leaders, dignitaries, and ordinary citizens visited Him and asked for His advice. Bahá'u'lláh frequently went to coffee houses, and whichever coffee house He chose would become crowded with people eager to meet with Him.

He showered love on many, giving gifts to the disabled, orphans, and others in need. When He went out, a poor, elderly woman would often wait for Him on the road. Bahá'u'lláh kindly asked about her health and gave her money. When she wanted to kiss His cheeks, He would bend down so she could do so. Later, when He left Baghdád, He arranged for an allowance to help her for the rest of her life.

Not everyone welcomed Bahá'u'lláh and the other Bábís. Some prejudiced people insulted and threatened them. At times, some Bábís got into conflicts with them. Bahá'u'lláh urged the Bábís to respond with patience and wisdom.

Once, some merchants even threatened to kill Bahá'u'lláh and the Bábís. But Bahá'u'lláh calmly went to the coffee house as usual. He told a companion, "We have been threatened with death. We have no fear, We are ready for them." He spoke with such authority that those who heard Him were amazed, and the merchants did not dare to hurt Him.

Another time, when more than 100 hostile men came to Bahá'u'lláh's house, He warmly invited them in and treated them with kind hospitality. In Bahá'u'lláh's presence, the men's hearts changed, and they left as friends.

Some people recognized Bahá'u'lláh's spiritual power and felt He was the Messenger of God promised by the Báb. In time, Bahá'u'lláh revealed that He was, indeed, the Promised One of all religions. The authorities exiled Him farther and farther from Persia, but they were unable to stop His profound effect on people's hearts and souls.

The statements above from Bahá'u'lláh are not authenticated quotations, but are His reported words from *Bahá'u'lláh: The King of Glory*, by H. M. Balyuzi.

The Life of Bahá'u'lláh

The highlighted area marks the time in which this story takes place.

Nobility of Navváb

Bahá'u'lláh and Ásíyih Khánum were married in 1835, when He was about 18. They both came from wealthy families. A jeweler worked for six months before the wedding to prepare Ásíyih Khánum's magnificent jewelry. Even her gold buttons were set with gems. It took 40 mules to carry her belongings.

Bahá'u'lláh gave His wife the title "Navváb," meaning "Grace" or "Highness." Like other wealthy, noble families, they could have enjoyed a life of luxury. But they chose a different path. They spent their time helping people in need.

In 1852, their lives were suddenly filled with danger and hardship. Because of His religion, Bahá'u'lláh was imprisoned. The family was forced from their home, and many of their possessions were stolen.

Navváb and her three children, who were all under nine years old, struggled to survive on their own. They worried about Bahá'u'lláh in the dark prison.

After about four months, Bahá'u'lláh was released—but He was banished from Persia (now Iran). Navváb sold gifts from her wedding to prepare for their travels through the mountains in the dead of winter to Baghdád, Iraq. She was expecting a baby, but she endured the rough journey without complaint. Only two of Bahá'u'lláh and Navváb's children made the trip: 'Abdu'l-Bahá and Bahíyyih Khánum. Mírzá Mihdí, the youngest, wasn't well enough to go. About seven years later, he joined his family.

In the following years, Navváb continued to share in Bahá'u'lláh's sufferings during His exiles to what are now Turkey and Israel.

Bahá'u'lláh's exile from His home in Tihrán, Persia (now Iran), covered about 3,000 miles (4,828 km).

She worked hard to care for her family. But the most difficult for Navváb was the loss of Mírzá Mihdí, who died in 'Akká, Israel, at age 22. He was pacing on the roof of the prison one evening, absorbed in devotions, when he fell through an open skylight.

In spite of many challenges, Bahíyyih Khánum said that her mother was "queenly in her dignity and loveliness, full of consideration for everybody, gentle, of a marvelous unselfishness, no action of hers ever failed to show the loving-kindness of her pure heart; her very presence seemed to make an atmosphere of love and happiness wherever she came, enfolding all comers in the fragrance of gentle courtesy."

In 1886, Navváb died in 'Akká, surrounded by her children and her beloved husband, Bahá'u'lláh, to whom she had been married for about 51 years.

Bahá'u'lláh wrote of Navváb, "We bear witness that thou didst attain unto all good, and that God hath so exalted thee, that all honor and glory circled around thee." Today, Bahá'ís from around the world pray at her resting place on Mount Carmel in Israel.

Messengers from One God

Who are your favorite teachers? Throughout our lives, our teachers introduce us to new ideas and valuable skills. They encourage us and challenge us to do our best. Humanity also has Teachers, sent by God throughout history, to help us learn and grow. These Teachers, or Messengers of God, include Moses, Buddha, Jesus, Muhammad, the Báb, and Bahá'u'lláh, among others. They are also known as Manifestations of God. Bahá'u'lláh wrote about Them in a book called the Kitáb-i-Íqán, which means "Book of Certitude" in Arabic.

The Báb had taught that another Messenger would soon appear to unite the world in peace. Authorities who wanted to end the new faith executed the Báb on July 9, 1850. More than 20,000 Bábís were killed over the years because of their beliefs.

Several of the Báb's family members were Bábís, but one of His uncles, Hájí Mírzá Siyyid Muhammad, did not believe in the Báb. In 1862, he went to Bahá'u'lláh in Baghdád and shared his doubts. Bahá'u'lláh told him to write down his questions. Then, in two days and nights, Bahá'u'lláh answered them, revealing a book over 200 pages long! He later named it the Kitáb-i-Íqán.

In the Kitáb-i-Íqán, Bahá'u'lláh explained the role of God's Messengers and praised Their lives and teachings. He described Them as Mirrors reflecting all of God's qualities, such as knowledge, wisdom, and glory. He wrote, "Human tongue can never befittingly sing their praise, and human speech can never unfold their mystery." He said prejudice caused many people to reject God's Messengers when They first appeared.

The Messengers of God, such as Krishna, Abraham, Moses, Buddha, Jesus, Muhammad, the Báb, and Bahá'u'lláh, are like different rays of the same sun.

Bahá'u'lláh wrote that although each Messenger of God has a different name and mission, They "are all sent down from the heaven of the Will of God, and as they all arise to proclaim His irresistible Faith, they therefore are regarded as one soul and the same person." Each religion is part of one unfolding faith from God. The Bahá'í writings say that although God's Messengers founded religions with some different laws and teachings, many essential truths remain the same. For example, the world's faiths teach us to treat others with kindness.

After reading Bahá'u'lláh's words in the Kitáb-i-Íqán, the Báb's uncle became a devoted believer in the Báb. Bahá'u'lláh later announced that He was the Messenger the Báb had promised. The Báb's uncle also declared his belief in Bahá'u'lláh.

Today, the Kitáb-i-Íqán still helps people understand God's Messengers. The Bahá'í writings describe it as "sweeping away the age-long barriers that have . . . separated the great religions of the world . . ." Bahá'u'lláh's teachings can bring peace and unity among people of all faiths by helping us see the oneness of all of God's Messengers.

Declaration in the Garden of Ridván

The Life of Bahá'u'lláh

The highlighted area marks the time in which this story takes place.

1817 November 12
Birth of Bahá'u'lláh in Tihrán, Iran

1844
Recognizes the Báb as a new Messenger of God

1852
Imprisonment in the "Black Pit" of Tihrán

1853–1863
Exile in Baghdád, Iraq. From 1854–1856, He goes into the mountains to pray in solitude.

1863 April
Declares Divine Mission as Prophet-Founder of the Bahá'í Faith

1863–1868
Exile in Constantinople (Istanbul), then Adrianople (Edirne), Turkey. Begins writing letters to kings and rulers in 1867, urging world unity

1868
Last exile, to prison-city of 'Akká, Israel

1877
Finally free to live in countryside homes of Mazra'ih and then Bahjí, outside 'Akká

1892 May 29
Bahá'u'lláh passes away at Bahjí.

Bahá'u'lláh and His family were exiled to Baghdád, Iraq, from their homeland in Persia (now Iran), because Muslim leaders wanted to diminish His influence as a leader in the Bábí Faith.

Many Bábís had been killed for their faith, and those living in Baghdád feared persecution. They didn't meet each other in public. But Bahá'u'lláh visited them and let people know that He was a Bábí. His courageous example inspired others, and they began to venture out. Soon people from all walks of life were drawn to Bahá'u'lláh's loving presence. They sought His wisdom and advice.

But in time, the Muslim authorities again felt threatened by Bahá'u'lláh's prominence in the city. In 1863, it was announced that He was being sent to Constantinople (now Istanbul, Turkey). Those who knew and loved Him were devastated. People flocked to His house to say goodbye, but His home was too small. A friend invited Him to use his garden on the Tigris River. Bahá'u'lláh and some of the Bábís gathered in the garden on April 22, 1863.

Bahá'u'lláh's departure was a sad occasion, but something amazing happened at that time. Bahá'u'lláh announced that He was the Promised Messenger of God foretold by the Báb. His followers were overjoyed. The farewell gathering became a wondrous spiritual occasion, and the garden became known as the Garden of Ridván ("Paradise" in Arabic).

Bahá'u'lláh wrote, "Rejoice with exceeding gladness, O people of Bahá, as ye call to remembrance the Day of supreme felicity, the Day whereon the Tongue of the Ancient of Days hath spoken, as He departed from His House, proceeding to the Spot from which He shed upon the whole of creation the splendors of His name, the All-Merciful."

For 12 days, Bahá'u'lláh met with friends who visited Him in the garden, including the governor, who admired Bahá'u'lláh and asked how he could help with His journey. Bahá'u'lláh asked that the Bábís in Baghdád be treated with kindness. The governor readily agreed.

Each day, gardeners would pick roses and place them in Bahá'u'lláh's tent. The flowers were piled so high that people couldn't see over them! Bahá'u'lláh had the roses taken to friends in Baghdád. At night, He walked and chanted prayers among the songs of nightingales.

Today, Bahá'ís joyfully celebrate the Festival of Ridván, which Bahá'u'lláh named the "Most Great Festival."

Bahá'u'lláh crossed the Tigris River to the rose-filled Garden of Ridván to say farewell to friends and to make a magnificent announcement.

"In the garden of thy heart plant naught but the rose of love . . ." —Bahá'u'lláh

In the rose bush, discover words related to the story of Bahá'u'lláh's declaration in the Garden of Riḍván. Fill in the blank roses with letters. Connected roses have the same letter.

Guidance for Global Leaders

The Life of Bahá'u'lláh

The highlighted area marks the time in which this story takes place.

1817 November 12
Birth of Bahá'u'lláh in Tihrán, Iran

1844
Recognizes the Báb as a new Messenger of God

1852
Imprisonment in the "Black Pit" of Tihrán

1853–1863
Exile in Baghdád, Iraq. From 1854–1856, He goes into the mountains to pray in solitude.

1863 April
Declares Divine Mission as Prophet-Founder of the Bahá'í Faith

1863–1868
Exile in Constantinople (Istanbul), then Adrianople (Edirne), Turkey. Begins writing letters to kings and rulers in 1867, urging world unity

1868
Last exile, to prison-city of 'Akká, Israel

1877
Finally free to live in countryside homes of Mazra'ih and then Bahjí, outside 'Akká

1892 May 29
Bahá'u'lláh passes away at Bahjí.

Envision being on a dangerous 12-day journey, riding in wagons or on pack animals. It's the middle of winter, and the bitter cold cuts through your thin clothes. The only way to get drinking water is to build a fire that melts the ice.

In 1863, Bahá'u'lláh, His family, and about a dozen companions faced these hardships. Though He had committed no crime, Muslim officials saw Bahá'u'lláh's influence as a threat, and He was exiled from Constantinople (now Istanbul) to Adrianople (now Edirne), Turkey.

Soon after Bahá'u'lláh arrived in Adrianople, people began noticing His noble character and kindness. Top officials, including the governor, visited Him. People bowed to Him in the streets.

A house of Bahá'u'lláh in Edirne, Turkey

Bahá'u'lláh spent much of His time revealing holy writings. "Day and night," wrote one eyewitness, "the Divine verses were raining down in such number that it was impossible to record them."

Although He was living in exile, Bahá'u'lláh fearlessly conveyed His teachings to some of the world's most powerful kings and leaders. He wrote to Sultán 'Abdu'l-'Azíz, who ruled the Ottoman Empire (including what are now Turkey and Israel), as well as to Násiri'd-Dín Sháh of Persia (now Iran), Czar Alexander II of Russia, Emperor Napoleon III of France, Queen Victoria of the United Kingdom, and Pope Pius IX. He also addressed Emperor Francis Joseph of Austria-Hungary, Kaiser William I of Germany, the rulers of the American continent, and all of the leaders on Earth as a group.

Bahá'u'lláh called upon these powerful people to turn to God and lead fairly. "Be vigilant, that ye may not do injustice to anyone," He wrote, "be it to the extent of a grain of mustard seed."

He told them to cooperate and establish peace on Earth. "Compose your differences, and reduce your armaments . . . that your minds and hearts may be tranquilized."

And He advised them to live moderately. "Your people are your treasures," He wrote. "Do not rob them to rear palaces for yourselves; nay rather choose for them that which ye choose for yourselves."

Some rulers responded angrily to Bahá'u'lláh. Napoleon reportedly flung away the first of two tablets he received, and ordered an impolite reply. Badí', a 17-year-old who voluntarily took Bahá'u'lláh's message to the sháh in Persia, was tortured and killed. Bahá'u'lláh later called him the "Pride of Martyrs."

Only Queen Victoria, whom Bahá'u'lláh praised for outlawing slavery, was open-minded. She was said to have noted, "If this is of God, it will endure; if not, it can do no harm."

Today, millions of Bahá'ís use Bahá'u'lláh's words as a blueprint for building peace and justice.

> "Tread ye the path of justice, for this, verily, is the straight path." —Bahá'u'lláh

Bahá'u'lláh called Adrianople the "remote prison." It was about 1,740 miles (2,800 km) from Tihrán, the farthest He was exiled from His homeland.

Find words from Bahá'u'lláh's tablets to the kings and rulers of the world.

DUTY
FAIRNESS
GENEROSITY
GRACE
HEAL
JUSTICE
KNOWLEDGE
MERCY
MIGHT
MODERATION
PEACE
POWER
PROTECT
SAFEGUARD
STEADFAST
TRUTH
UNITY
WISDOM

```
M O D E R A T I O N N Y Y S
S E T M A K P H Y B T C T S
A T C G E V N Y T I Y E I C
F L E I R R T O S U A E N H
E O T P T U C O W D R Y U U
G M O Z D S R Y F L W T M N
U I R T Y E U A N K E O A X
A G P O N S S J Z M D D U K
R H Z E I T P T F S A N G W
D T G S S E N R I A F Z H E
H E A L A Y B W G R A C E O
Q C J C R E W O P O H X Z L
N S E Z H W L W M P L R B J
A M K L V J Z A L Q Z A L U
```

'Akká, the Prison-City

The Life of Bahá'u'lláh

The highlighted area marks the time in which this story takes place.

1817 November 12
Birth of Bahá'u'lláh in Tihrán, Iran

1844
Recognizes the Báb as a new Messenger of God

1852
Imprisonment in the "Black Pit" of Tihrán

1853–1863
Exile in Baghdád, Iraq. From 1854–1856, He goes into the mountains to pray in solitude.

1863 April
Declares Divine Mission as Prophet-Founder of the Bahá'í Faith

1863–1868
Exile in Constantinople (Istanbul), then Adrianople (Edirne), Turkey. Begins writing letters to kings and rulers in 1867, urging world unity

1868
Last exile, to prison-city of 'Akká, Israel

1877
Finally free to live in countryside homes of Mazra'ih and then Bahjí, outside 'Akká

1892 May 29
Bahá'u'lláh passes away at Bahjí.

There was almost no wind as the blazing August sun beat down on the small sailboat in Haifa Bay during eight miserable hours. Bahá'u'lláh and about 70 companions, including His family, endured the terrible journey to 'Akká, in what is now Israel, in 1868. Muslim authorities felt threatened by Bahá'u'lláh's religious teachings. They thought that by sending Him to 'Akká, they could stop the Bahá'í Faith from spreading.

When the exiles arrived at the sea gate in 'Akká, they had to wade through the water to enter the city. The men were ordered to carry the women on their backs, but Bahá'u'lláh's eldest son, 'Abdu'l-Bahá, insisted that the women be treated with dignity. He managed to get a chair, and each woman was carried respectfully over the water.

'Akká was a desolate prison-city of about 9,000. It was said that birds flying over the city would drop dead from the stench. 'Akká's inhabitants had been told that Bahá'u'lláh and His followers were evil criminals who deserved cruel treatment. When the exiles entered the city, they were met with jeers from the crowd.

The Bahá'ís were led to an old army barracks that served as their prison. Conditions were dire. It was so hot and foul-smelling that Bahá'u'lláh's daughter, Bahíyyih Khánum, fainted. They were given nothing to eat or drink the first night. The next day each person finally received water and a few loaves of salty bread. All but two of them became ill. Three men died, including two brothers who died in each other's arms.

Bahá'u'lláh said of the imprisonment

Bahá'u'lláh and His companions arrived at the sea gate in 'Akká in 1868.

in 'Akká, "None knoweth what befell Us, except God, the Almighty, the All-Knowing . . . From the foundation of the world until the present day a cruelty such as this hath neither been seen nor heard of."

Three days after their arrival, the judgment from the Ottoman ruler, Sultán 'Abdu'l-'Azíz, was read at the mosque. Bahá'u'lláh was sentenced to life imprisonment. The Bahá'ís were not allowed to associate with anyone.

However, despite the vicious rumors about the Bahá'ís, some citizens of 'Akká recognized Bahá'u'lláh's noble character. One man among the hostile crowd, Khalíl Ahmad 'Abdú, said he could see in Bahá'u'lláh's face signs of greatness, majesty, and truthfulness. He said that the people of 'Akká should be thankful to God for Bahá'u'lláh's presence in their city. Another man, 'Abdu'lláh Tuzih, saw radiance, power, and glory in Bahá'u'lláh. He later became a Bahá'í.

In time, others grew to respect Bahá'u'lláh and the Bahá'ís. 'Abdu'l-Bahá became known for his care and concern

"Consort with the followers of all religions in a spirit of friendliness and fellowship." —Bahá'u'lláh

for others, especially those who were poor or sick. Bahá'u'lláh's strength and integrity impressed the authorities, and they gradually eased the harsh restrictions. He was eventually given the freedom to leave the prison-city and live in the nearby countryside.

Bahá'u'lláh spent His final years at Bahjí, near 'Akká. After His passing, a shrine was built at His resting place. Bahá'ís around the world consider it the holiest spot on Earth.

Bahjí, the home where Bahá'u'lláh spent the final years of His life, is near 'Akká, Israel.

Bahá'u'lláh urged us to live together in peace. Use the key to decode His words.

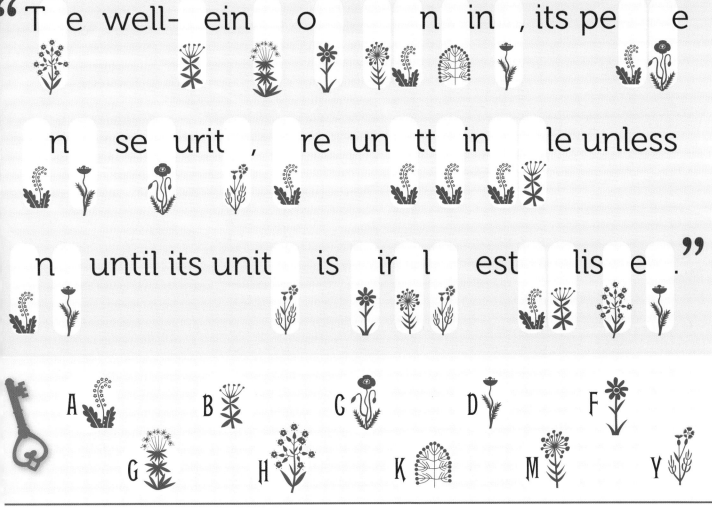

"T e well- ein o n in , its pe e n se urit , re un tt in le unless n until its unit is ir l est lis e ."

31

A Brief
Timeline

The Life of
Bahá'u'lláh

The highlighted
area marks the
time in which this
story takes place.

1817 November 12
Birth of Bahá'u'lláh
in Tihrán, Iran

1844
Recognizes the Báb as
a new Messenger of God

1852
Imprisonment in the
"Black Pit" of Tihrán

1853–1863
Exile in Baghdád, Iraq.
From 1854–1856, He
goes into the mountains
to pray in solitude.

1863 April
Declares Divine Mission
as Prophet-Founder
of the Bahá'í Faith

1863–1868
Exile in Constantinople
(Istanbul), then Adrianople
(Edirne), Turkey. Begins
writing letters to kings
and rulers in 1867,
urging world unity

1868
Last exile, to prison-
city of 'Akká, Israel

1877
Finally free to live in
countryside homes
of Mazra'ih and then
Bahjí, outside 'Akká

1892 May 29
Bahá'u'lláh passes
away at Bahjí.

Miracles and Mysteries

Have you ever heard of mysterious or miraculous events and wondered if they're true? The history of religion is full of such stories, including this one from the Bahá'í writings about Mírzá Ja'far-i-Yazdí. He was a religious scholar in the city of Yazd, Persia (now Iran). When he learned about the Bahá'í Faith, he accepted it wholeheartedly. He traveled to Baghdád, Iraq, and met Bahá'u'lláh. Mírzá Ja'far decided to give up his position and instead work as a carpenter and as a servant for Bahá'u'lláh's house-hold. He felt content to humbly serve Bahá'u'lláh, His family, and the other Bahá'ís.

In 1868, when Bahá'u'lláh and about 70 family members and friends were exiled to 'Akká, in what is now Israel, Mírzá Ja'far was among them. Though they had not committed any crime, they were sent to the foul prison-city because the government wanted to stop Bahá'u'lláh's teachings of unity from spreading.

After arriving in 'Akká, Mírzá Ja'far became terribly ill. His condition grew worse and worse, until the doctor said he could do nothing more to help him. Finally, Mírzá Ja'far stopped breathing, and his body went limp and cold. Family and friends surrounded him, weeping and mourning his death. Another Bahá'í, Mírzá Áqá Ján, ran to Bahá'u'lláh and told Him of Mírzá Ja'far's passing. Bahá'u'lláh said to him, "Go; chant the prayer of Yá Sháfí—O Thou, the Healer—and Mírzá Ja'far will come alive. Very rapidly, he will be as well as ever."

The prayer was chanted. Mírzá Ja'far began to stir. Slowly, he started to move his limbs. Within an hour, he was sitting up, laughing and telling jokes with his friends!

Mírzá Ja'far was imprisoned for his faith in 'Akká, Israel, with Bahá'u'lláh and many of His followers. While in prison, Mírzá Ja'far lived through a very mysterious experience.

He lived a long time after that, continuing to assist Bahá'u'lláh and the Bahá'ís.

Messengers of God, such as Moses, Jesus, Muhammad, the Báb, and Bahá'u'lláh, had the power to cause miracles. While stories such as this are remarkable, the Bahá'í writings say that these accounts should not be seen as proof of God's Messengers.

'Abdu'l-Bahá, Bahá'u'lláh's son who led the Bahá'í Faith after His passing, said, "many marvelous things appeared from Bahá'u'lláh, but . . . they are not . . . a decisive proof . . ." He also explained that to the Messengers of God, "these miracles and wonderful signs have no importance . . . They are still only proofs and arguments for those who are present when they are performed, and not for those who are absent." He explained that miracles also have spiritual meanings.

The true proof of the Messengers of God is in Their words. When Their teachings have the ability to change people's hearts and inspire them to be of service to others—that is the real miracle.

Seeing with Your Own Eyes

Backbiting and gossip can spread like wildfire and be just as destructive. Like smoke from a fire, rumors can cloud your vision. How do you clear the air to see the truth for yourself?

Rumors raged among the citizens of 'Akká that the Bahá'ís were terrible criminals. Because of these rumors, most people in 'Akká treated the Bahá'ís with suspicion and hate. When they arrived, a crowd gathered to jeer and mock them.

After being imprisoned for over two years, Bahá'u'lláh and most of His family were moved to different houses, then crowded into a house too small for them.

Soon after, a conflict erupted among some of the exiles who did not follow Bahá'u'lláh's teachings. This intensified hostility from the people of 'Akká. Ilyás 'Abbúd, whose house was attached to Bahá'u'lláh's, barricaded the walls that separated the homes. Bahá'í children were chased and even pelted with stones.

Some of the Bahá'ís were imprisoned at an inn in the city. Soldiers who kept guard over them treated them harshly. However, the gentle and patient character of the Bahá'ís began to change the guards' hearts. They admitted that they had been prejudiced by the rumors. The guards became friendlier, and the Bahá'ís even had them in for tea. The soldiers soon believed that the authorities were unfair for imprisoning the Bahá'ís. Finally, they boldly refused to stand guard over people they saw as peaceful.

Bahá'u'lláh and about 70 family members and followers lived in this prison in 'Akká for over two years.

Bahá'ís changed the hearts of the prison guards of 'Akká.

Ilyás 'Abbúd also had a big change of heart after living next to the Bahá'ís and seeing their behavior. He tore down his barricades, and he even offered his own home to Bahá'u'lláh and His family!

Over time, others in 'Akká began to see with their own eyes that the rumors about the Bahá'ís were false. A new governor came to 'Akká who treated the Bahá'ís with kindness. He admired Bahá'u'lláh's son, 'Abdu'l-Bahá, so much that he removed his shoes in 'Abdu'l-Bahá's presence out of respect. He even sent his own son to be taught by 'Abdu'l-Bahá. When Bahá'u'lláh met him, the governor begged for the opportunity to do some service for Him. Bahá'u'lláh suggested that the governor repair the city's aqueduct, which hadn't functioned for 30 years, so fresh water could flow to the city. The governor began the project immediately.

Life in 'Akká had started out terribly for the Bahá'ís. But after the conflicts, rumors, and lies settled, many saw the true nature of Bahá'u'lláh and His teachings.

A Brief Timeline

The Life of Bahá'u'lláh

The highlighted area marks the time in which this story takes place.

1817 November 12
Birth of Bahá'u'lláh in Tihrán, Iran

1844
Recognizes the Báb as a new Messenger of God

1852
Imprisonment in the "Black Pit" of Tihrán

1853–1863
Exile in Baghdád, Iraq. From 1854–1856, He goes into the mountains to pray in solitude.

1863 April
Declares Divine Mission as Prophet-Founder of the Bahá'í Faith

1863–1868
Exile in Constantinople (Istanbul), then Adrianople (Edirne), Turkey. Begins writing letters to kings and rulers in 1867, urging world unity

1868
Last exile, to prison-city of 'Akká, Israel

1877
Finally free to live in countryside homes of Mazra'ih and then Bahjí, outside 'Akká

1892 May 29
Bahá'u'lláh passes away at Bahjí.

A Change of Heart

Mahmúd was a 10-year-old boy who lived in 'Akká, in what is now Israel, long ago. One day, a wise old man told Mahmúd about a vision he'd had. The man said that the next Messenger of God would come to 'Akká when Mahmúd was an adult. The Messenger would speak Persian, and He would live in a room at the top of a long flight of stairs.

When Mahmúd grew up, he became respected in the community as a religious leader.

One day, Mahmúd learned that a prisoner, Bahá'u'lláh, had arrived in 'Akká. Mahmúd was angry that Bahá'u'lláh had been sent to his city. Hatred poisoned his heart. He wanted so desperately to rid 'Akká of a person he considered "evil" that he decided to kill Bahá'u'lláh.

One day, Mahmúd hid a weapon under his cloak and went to the prison where Bahá'u'lláh was held. But when the guard announced Mahmúd, Bahá'u'lláh said, "Tell him to cast away the weapon and then he may come in." Mahmúd was stunned. He was sure no one had seen his weapon. He turned and left, confused.

Shaken, but still determined, Mahmúd returned to the prison empty-handed. He was strong, and he decided he could kill Bahá'u'lláh with his bare hands. Once again, the guard announced his visit. This time, Bahá'u'lláh replied, "Tell him to purify his heart first and then he may come in." Mahmúd was so perplexed that he left without seeing Bahá'u'lláh.

Later, Mahmúd had a dream about the old man he had met as a child. He remembered the man's mysterious vision. After his dream, Mahmúd returned to the prison. He met with Bahá'u'lláh's son, 'Abdu'l-Bahá, whose words changed him. This time, Mahmúd was brought to Bahá'u'lláh's cell at the top of a long flight of stairs. Overwhelmed by Bahá'u'lláh's presence, Mahmúd fell to his knees. He became a devoted Bahá'í for the rest of his life.

He helped Bahá'ís enter and leave 'Akká to visit Bahá'u'lláh. Sometimes he even had ropes lowered so Bahá'ís could be pulled up over the walls that surrounded the city.

Mahmúd was one of many people who approached Bahá'u'lláh as an enemy, but then grew to admire Him. Though authorities tried to stop His influence, no one could prevent Bahá'u'lláh's love and wisdom from changing people's hearts.

These are the reported words of Bahá'u'lláh and may not be exact quotations

A Mysterious Tablet

Imagine having a wish granted—before you even wish it! That happened to a historian and teacher named Hájí Muhammad-Tahír.

While Bahá'u'lláh was imprisoned in 'Akká (now in Israel), the Hájí came from Yazd, Persia (now Iran) to visit Him.

The Hájí met with Bahá'u'lláh every other day for nine months. He was so overwhelmed by Bahá'u'lláh's majesty that he could barely look at Him or speak a word. Once, when he gazed at Bahá'u'lláh's face, he was so awed that he spilled a cup of hot tea on himself without noticing it.

The Hájí wrote, "Whenever I came into the presence of the Blessed Beauty if there were anything I wanted to ask, I would say it by way of the heart and He would answer me invariably. I was so deeply impressed by His supreme power that I always sat in His presence spell-bound, oblivious of myself."

Hájí Muhammad-Tahír longed for a tablet—or even a few words—written in Bahá'u'lláh's own handwriting. He had heard that one of the Báb's teachings was that even a word written by Bahá'u'lláh was a precious treasure. But he did not request it. One day, Bahá'u'lláh told him that He *had* revealed a tablet for him, but he would receive it in the future. Hájí Muhammad-Tahír was elated.

Hájí Muhammad-Tahír

When he returned to Yazd, the Hájí taught many about the Bahá'í Faith. He was a brilliant speaker and knowledgeable about the Qur'án, the Bible, and other holy books. But officials did not want him to spread Bahá'u'lláh's teachings. After some years, a death warrant was issued for the Hájí, and he decided to leave Yazd.

As the Hájí mounted his donkey in the dark of night, a devoted Bahá'í woman approached and handed him something. It was a tablet in Bahá'u'lláh's handwriting! The woman had received it 24 years earlier, when Bahá'u'lláh was in Baghdád—long before He was imprisoned in 'Akká. Bahá'u'lláh had said that its rightful owner would be known later. The woman knew in her heart that the tablet was for the Hájí. He accepted it with deep joy. Bahá'u'lláh had written it when the Hájí was a child, before they had met in person!

Hájí Muhammad-Tahír was so inspired by Bahá'u'lláh that he shared the Bahá'í Faith with hundreds of people. Though he was persecuted and imprisoned, he remained faithful until the end of his life, at about 100.

Our Green Island

The Life of Bahá'u'lláh

The highlighted area marks the time in which this story takes place.

1817 November 12
Birth of Bahá'u'lláh in Tihrán, Iran

1844
Recognizes the Báb as a new Messenger of God

1852
Imprisonment in the "Black Pit" of Tihrán

1853–1863
Exile in Baghdád, Iraq. From 1854–1856, He goes into the mountains to pray in solitude.

1863 April
Declares Divine Mission as Prophet-Founder of the Bahá'í Faith

1863–1868
Exile in Constantinople (Istanbul), then Adrianople (Edirne), Turkey. Begins writing letters to kings and rulers in 1867, urging world unity

1868
Last exile, to prison-city of 'Akká, Israel

1877
Finally free to live in countryside homes of Mazra'ih and then Bahjí, outside 'Akká

1892 May 29
Bahá'u'lláh passes away at Bahjí.

From the small window of His prison cell, Bahá'u'lláh could see a stone wall, and beyond it, the Mediterranean Sea. Then, after moving from the prison to a house in the city, Bahá'u'lláh had only the narrow, filthy streets of 'Akká (now in Israel) to gaze upon each day.

One day, Bahá'u'lláh noted that He hadn't seen greenery in nine years. His son, 'Abdu'l-Bahá, rented a garden outside of 'Akká for Him.

In 1877, Bahá'u'lláh was allowed to move to the countryside, although He was still a prisoner. He enjoyed the garden, with scents of jasmine and orange blossoms filling the air. Bahá'u'lláh named it Ridván ("Paradise"). He also called it "Our Green Island" and described "its streams flowing, and its trees luxuriant, and the sunlight playing in their midst." He wrote about a divine vision in "that most sublime, that blest, and most exalted Spot."

The Ridván Garden has been restored to look as it did in Bahá'u'lláh's day. You can imagine the joy and peace of being in Bahá'u'lláh's presence in that beautiful place.

Imagine the Ridván Garden as you search for these words. Look forward, backward, up, down, and diagonally.

```
Y R R E B L U M T B C D
M T N A I R U X U L B Q
Q B I M E C G B O O P B
L S P L N X Q K S E Q
F J H M I N H I I S G V
V O S W M U S H P O X F
R N O M S L Q G G A M W V
T L T Z A U R N R S G J
F H D N J E N L A A V G
E T D R E D R L D R S Y
O I V N Q D E T I N T O
A U J E U Z R N S G W P
G W S Q Y T U A E B H H
J P E U A R T C G K T T
D T B G G E A X N N O S
R W V G B E N Y A C G X
D T U C P S J Q R P L I
G Q C A B Q C O O K Z F
```

TREES • GARDEN • ORANGES • MULBERRY • FLOWING • BEAUTY • SUNLIGHT • NATURE • BLOSSOMS • JASMINE • LUXURIANT • PARADISE • ISLAND • GREEN • PEACE • TRANQUILITY • STREAMS

What if you couldn't see trees or plants for nine long years? This happened to Bahá'u'lláh, Who loved nature from childhood. Officials who wanted to stop His new religion sent Him to the prison-city of 'Akká, in what is now Israel. From 1868 to 1877, He didn't see a single blade of grass.

When Bahá'u'lláh was finally released, He visited a beautiful garden that His son, 'Abdu'l-Bahá, and others had prepared for Him outside of 'Akká. The fragrant flowers and fruit trees brought Bahá'u'lláh great joy. He wrote, "Every tree uttered a word, and every leaf sang a melody." He called it Ridván, which means "Paradise" in Arabic.

One day, a swarm of locusts began eating the trees. The gardener, Abu'l-Qásim, was distraught. Bahá'u'lláh smiled and said, "The locusts must be fed; let them be." Still, Abu'l-Qásim was upset to see the destruction, and he begged Bahá'u'lláh to do something.

Bahá'u'lláh then said to the locusts, "Abu'l-Qásim does not want you; God protect you." He shook the hem of His robe, and the locusts flew away. To this day, the Ridván Garden remains a paradise for all who visit it.

What virtues help us care for nature? Discover some in the Garden of Ridván. Fill in the blank oranges with letters. Connected oranges have the same letter.

For Love and Unity

The Life of Bahá'u'lláh

The highlighted area marks the time in which this story takes place.

1817 November 12
Birth of Bahá'u'lláh in Tihrán, Iran

1844
Recognizes the Báb as a new Messenger of God

1852
Imprisonment in the "Black Pit" of Tihrán

1853–1863
Exile in Baghdád, Iraq. From 1854–1856, He goes into the mountains to pray in solitude.

1863 April
Declares Divine Mission as Prophet-Founder of the Bahá'í Faith

1863–1868
Exile in Constantinople (Istanbul), then Adrianople (Edirne), Turkey. Begins writing letters to kings and rulers in 1867, urging world unity

1868
Last exile, to prison-city of 'Akká, Israel

1877
Finally free to live in countryside homes of Mazra'ih and then Bahjí, outside 'Akká

1892 May 29
Bahá'u'lláh passes away at Bahjí.

For more than half of His life, Bahá'u'lláh lived as a prisoner and an exile. During His divine mission to spread God's message of unity and peace, authorities who were prejudiced against Him tried to stop Him—but they were unsuccessful. In spite of their efforts, Bahá'u'lláh won the hearts of people from all walks of life.

In 1877, Bahá'u'lláh was able to leave the prison-city of 'Akká, in what is now Israel. He moved to a nearby countryside mansion for two years. Then He lived in the Mansion of Bahjí, closer to 'Akká, for nearly 13 years, revealing holy writings and meeting with visitors.

About a week before He left this world, Bahá'u'lláh gathered His family and followers. He said, "I am well pleased with you all. Ye have rendered many services, and been very assiduous in your labors. Ye have come here every morning and every evening. May God assist you to remain united."

After a brief illness, Bahá'u'lláh passed away on May 29, 1892, at the age of 74. Just after sunset on that day, He was buried in a small stone house next to the mansion.

Friends from various religions and backgrounds, including government officials, came to grieve with Bahá'u'lláh's family. Many could be seen weeping in the fields surrounding the mansion. Some wrote tributes to Him. The family generously served food to all the mourning visitors.

Nine days after His passing, Bahá'u'lláh's Will and Testament was unsealed. In it, He told His followers to turn to His son, 'Abdu'l-Bahá, for guidance. Only 'Abdu'l-Bahá was authorized to interpret Bahá'u'lláh's writings. This was the first time in known history

Bahá'ís from all over the world travel to Israel for pilgrimage, a highlight of which is praying at the Shrine of Bahá'u'lláh.

that the Founder of a world religion had clearly stated whom people should follow after His death. It ensured that His faith would remain united, instead of splitting into sects, and that His followers would not argue over who would lead them.

In His will, Bahá'u'lláh wrote that His aim had been "to quench the flame of hate and enmity, that the horizon of the hearts of men may be illumined with the light of concord and attain real peace and tranquility." He also urged, "The religion of God is for love and unity; make it not the cause of enmity or dissension." Bahá'u'lláh's final wishes reflected His mission to unify all people.

Over the years, 'Abdu'l-Bahá and his grandson, Shoghi Effendi, beautified the gardens around Bahá'u'lláh's shrine. It is the holiest place on Earth for Bahá'ís, and the place toward which they turn in prayer each day. Today, more than five million Bahá'ís are working to share Bahá'u'lláh's message of peace and create a more harmonious world.

GROW YOUR SOUL

Just as a seed can become a mighty tree, each of us can grow to become active, fruitful spirits in our families, communities, and schools. Bahá'u'lláh said, "Sow the seeds of My divine wisdom in the pure soil of the heart . . ."

When we act with kindness, meditate, read sacred writings, and pray, it's like watering the seeds in our hearts. Our spiritual qualities will grow and blossom, and our daily actions can lead to great harvests in our journey through life.

ACTS OF KINDNESS

★ Invite a friend to dinner or to a fun event.

★ Say a prayer for someone who's having a tough time.

★ Tell a friend what you appreciate about them.

★ Create a homemade thank-you card for your teacher.

★ Do a kind deed in secret for a family member or neighbor.

★ Start a service project that you can do with your friends or family.

★ Bake a treat for a neighbor or worker in your community.

★ Start a conversation with a kid at school who's sitting alone.

★ Ask your family how you can be helpful at home.

★ Be a good listener.

★ Smile and wave at your neighbors.

★ Say "thank you" when someone does something kind for you.

MEDITATION

★ Go outside and appreciate the trees, plants, flowers, sun, and other gifts in God's creation.

★ Find a quiet place, close your eyes, and focus on breathing slowly and deeply.

★ Stretch your body or do yoga poses while calming your mind.

★ Imagine a peaceful place in nature, such as a beach or forest.

★ Gaze at the clouds or stars and ponder the amazing universe.

★ Read writings from different religions and think about their meanings.

★ List 10 things you're grateful for.

★ Savor a happy memory. Think about the sights, sounds, smells, feelings, and people you enjoyed.

★ Silently repeat a word or phrase that has meaning to you, such as "love" or "Alláh-u-Abhá" ("God the All-Glorious" in Arabic).

PRAYERS

O God, guide me, protect me, make of me a shining lamp and a brilliant star. Thou art the Mighty and the Powerful.
—'Abdu'l-Bahá

O my God! O my God! Unite the hearts of Thy servants, and reveal to them Thy great purpose. May they follow Thy commandments and abide in Thy law. Help them, O God, in their endeavor, and grant them strength to serve Thee. O God! Leave them not to themselves, but guide their steps by the light of Thy knowledge, and cheer their hearts by Thy love. Verily, Thou art their Helper and their Lord.
—Bahá'u'lláh

The Life of Bahá'u'lláh
A TREASURY OF STORIES FROM Brilliant Star

CREDITS

Author: Annie Reneau

Illustrator: C. Aaron Kreader

Senior Editor: Amy Renshaw

Editor/Creative Director: Amethel Parel-Sewell

Production Support: Lisa Blecker, Susan Engle, Foad Ghorbani, Heidi Parsons, Donna Price

Historical photos courtesy of Bahá'í World Center, Bahá'í International Community, and U.S. Bahá'í National Archives

Photos on pages 6, 12, 16, and 19 by Effie Baker; page 7 photo by Axel Anders; page 18 art by Foad Ghorbani; page 19 calligraphy by Burhan Zahrai; page 24 story by Susan Engle; page 28 photo by Dean Wilkey; page 36 inking and watercoloring by Lisa Blecker

Licensed from Shutterstock: running graphics by New Line, Pashabo, Marilyn Volan; page 3 stamp by Aquir; page 4 by Double Brain; pages 5 and 40 by Maljuk; page 24 map base by Frees; page 25 by Creative Travel Projects; page 26 by Marzolino

Brilliant Star
A BAHÁ'Í COMPANION FOR YOUNG EXPLORERS
www.brilliantstarmagazine.org

BAHÁ'Í PUBLISHING
Bahá'í Publishing is an imprint of the Bahá'í Publishing Trust of the United States.
http://BahaiBookstore.com

ACTIVITY ANSWERS

Page 9: 1) charity, 2) appreciation, 3) faith, 4) generosity, 5) kindness, 6) enthusiasm, 7) service, 8) courage, 9) thankfulness

Page 13: "Ye are the fruits of one tree, and the leaves of one branch. Deal ye one with another with the utmost love and harmony..."

Page 21: "To be poor in all save God is a wondrous gift . . . for in the end it will make thee rich in God."

Page 27: Mystery, community, celebration, friendship, festival, nightingales, garden, promise, joyous, paradise

Page 31: "The well-being of mankind, its peace and security, are unattainable unless and until its unity is firmly established."

Page 37: Respect, moderation, gratitude, cooperation, responsibility, optimism, commitment, creativity, awareness, compassion